The Fourth Estate

Journalism in North America

Internet Journalism and Fake News

Jonathan S. Adams

Cavendish Square

New York

Published in 2019 by Cavendish Square Publishing, LLC
243 5th Avenue, Suite 136, New York, NY 10016

Library of Congress Cataloging-in-Publication Data

Names: Adams, Jonathan S., 1961- author.
Title: Internet Journalism and Fake News / Jonathan S. Adams.
Description: New York : Cavendish Square, 2018. | Series: The Fourth Estate:
Journalism in North America | Includes bibliographical references and index.
Identifiers: LCCN 2017058841 (print) | LCCN 2017060442 (ebook) | ISBN 9781502634962 (eBook) |
ISBN 9781502634955 (library bound) | ISBN 9781502634979 (pbk.) | ISBN 9781502634986 (6 pack)
Subjects: LCSH: Online journalism--United States. | Citizen
journalism--United States. | Fake news--United States.
Classification: LCC PN4867.2 (ebook) | LCC PN4867.2 .A33 2018 (print) | DDC 070.4--dc23
LC record available at https://lccn.loc.gov/2017058841

Editorial Director: David McNamara
Editor: Caitlyn Miller
Copy Editor: Nathan Heidelberger
Associate Art Director: Amy Greenan
Designer: Joe Parenteau
Production Coordinator: Karol Szymczuk
Photo Research: J8 Media

Printed in the United States of America

CONTENTS

News is now available everywhere we go, courtesy of mobile technology that was inconceivable a few decades ago.

Journalism in the Digital Age

Most everyone today carries a smartphone that is millions of times more powerful than the computers that astronauts used to fly to the moon and back for the first time. Each one of these tiny computers is a piece of technology that was incomprehensible just a few decades ago. Moreover, smartphones serve as a link to the most incredible compilation of information in all human history.

That compilation grows literally by the second. Everyone with a smartphone or laptop is instantly connected to as much news, information, and data as they can consume. And people no longer just consume news. They now report and comment on it too, using high-resolution cameras to capture events as they happen, posting their views instantly on services like Twitter, or publishing essays and articles on their own blogs. The line between journalism and citizenship is blurring. News is available everywhere, all of the time, in multiple formats that we can tailor to our liking.

The scope of the revolution in the way we get, process, and understand information about current events and the world around us can hardly be overstated. This book traces the emergence of a new kind of journalism driven—and in some cases overtaken—by rapidly changing information technologies. These technologies have implications not only for the profession of journalism but also for anyone seeking to make informed decisions in an ever more connected world. The new journalism of the twenty-first century also raises important questions about how we separate what is important from what is not, and what is true from what is false.

Newspapers and the Dawn of the Digital Age

Two key moments for the practice of modern journalism occurred in 1984. One marked the beginning of a long, slow trend that continues to this day and hence went largely unnoticed at the time. The other lasted for just one minute, but in that short time it established an unmistakable place in the history of American media, culture, and technology.

The trend was in the number of people who read daily newspapers in the United States. That number reached its peak in 1984, at just over sixty-three million. The number had climbed steadily for decades, reflecting the entrenched position of the daily newspaper in the United States, particularly in big cities.

Though no one could have known it at the time, 1984 marked the beginning of the end of that era. Daily circulation numbers remained near their high-water mark until the end of the decade (and circulation for Sunday papers actually grew throughout that period), but they would never again exceed sixty-three million. An accelerating downward trend began in the early 1990s and has continued ever since. By 2016, the estimated daily circulation of newspapers in the United States was down to less than thirty-five million, a decrease of more than 44 percent.

A large part of the reason for this downward trend was captured perfectly by the other significant media event of 1984. On January 22, CBS aired a commercial during the Super Bowl for a new personal computer, the Apple Macintosh. The commercial opens in a dark, industrial setting, with rows of identically dressed people marching through a long tunnel and gathering before an enormous television screen. On the screen is a close-up of an imposing man giving a stern, almost angry speech.

Then, a woman dressed in brightly colored athletic gear and carrying a large hammer sprints down the aisle, pursued by police officers. As she nears the screen, she hurls her hammer, and the screen explodes in a flurry of light and smoke. Then the following words appear: "On January 24th, Apple Computer will introduce Macintosh. And you'll see why 1984 won't be like '1984.'"

The ad, known simply as "1984," aired on national television only once. But millions of people saw it, and it has been replayed countless times ever since. It has been called one of the greatest commercials ever made. The ad marks a crucial turning point: the beginning of the age of personal computers. Apple had neither invented nor perfected the technology behind personal computers,

Steve Wozniak (*left*) and Steve Jobs (*center*), cofounders of Apple, along with company president John Scully, with the Apple Macintosh personal computer on April 24, 1984

but its ad sought to capture their potential to make information available on an unheard-of scale. Personal computers have changed many aspects of American society. Some of the most profound changes have occurred in the way people in this country consume and share news.

The Rise of the Personal Computer

The technology behind those changes emerged slowly at first and then, in the mid-1980s, explosively. In the 1960s, an arm of the United States military called the Advanced Research Projects Agency (ARPA) began looking at how to link widely separated computers. With time, the project went beyond the military and connected large computers at universities for academic purposes. They were able to link four computers (three in California and one in Utah) by late 1969. By 1981, there were over two hundred links in what was then known as ARPANET.

That marked a significant technical achievement, but hardly anyone outside of the military or academic research institutions knew anything about it. The idea that a large number of people would have computers at home that would enable them to access ARPANET or anything like it was considered by many experts to be absurd. After all, early computers took up entire rooms.

The consensus opinion was that computers would always be too big, expensive, and complicated for widespread use. However, not everyone agreed. Small companies, among them Radio Shack, Commodore, and Apple, saw an opportunity and began to develop computers that were powerful, easy to use, and

A Commodore personal computer, circa 1980. Commodore, Apple, and Radio Shack were among the small companies that saw the potential of the personal computer market in the early 1980s.

inexpensive enough for average consumers rather than skilled technicians and large institutions. Then, the biggest technology company at the time, IBM, joined the race. The personal computer, or PC, was born.

The question of how to put computers in the hands of millions of people was in the process of being answered. The question of what they could do with those machines remained.

Early Experiments in Digital News

Newspaper publishers were well aware of new digital technologies on the horizon. Publishers began experimenting with ways to get beyond print well before the PC became mainstream. However, the ideas behind these experiments were too far ahead of the technology itself. Too few people owned computers, and those who did owned machines that were not powerful enough to take advantage of the information the newspaper publishers were trying to deliver.

While few people owned a computer, nearly everyone had a television. The earliest efforts to take advantage of new technologies built on this fact. Media companies invested in providing low-cost "decoder" boxes that delivered text and graphics to TV screens. In 1970, a company in the United Kingdom invented a system called teletext that allowed television viewers to punch numbers into a remote control to select various pages of information from menus on their screen. The system had significant limitations, though. News and information had to be brief, often just one hundred words. It could be slow to load the pages. The graphics were poor. Teletext never caught on.

The next step in the evolution was called videotex, and it was the forerunner of all interactive, online media. Like teletext, the system was originally designed for televisions rather than computers. But unlike teletext, the new technology was interactive, allowing two-way communication between consumers and companies providing information. A set-top box received information from a database via a telephone line or a TV cable. Users selected what they wanted to see using a dedicated keyboard.

By the early 1980s videotex gained traction, particularly in France, where it remained in use until 2012. Some major American newspaper companies took notice of that success. They saw an opportunity to build their own systems using the same technology. One such effort was an ambitious project known as Viewtron, developed as a joint effort between two giant corporations: AT&T and newspaper publisher Knight Ridder.

Viewtron launched in 1980. In a promotional video, the companies billed it as one of the most important technological advances in human history. The service would be the cure for what the companies called "information overload" and would give users instant access to "virtually unlimited information," including news, weather, banking, and shopping.

Viewtron eventually spread to fifteen cities. Yet like its predecessor, Viewtron never caught on. It required users to buy an expensive terminal and pay an additional monthly fee. The devices tied up the home TV and telephone and were not designed to handle large volumes of electronic messages.

Knight Ridder scrapped Viewtron after just six years, at a loss of more than $70 million. It has been called one of the biggest information technology failures ever. The company returned to its core newspaper business rather than pursuing other opportunities from the emerging use of PCs. Some smaller companies, however, were already testing the waters.

An important step was the development of the bulletin board system (BBS), which could deliver information to personal computers rather than televisions. In 1990, the *Albuquerque Tribune* launched a news service that used BBS software and telephone lines to provide digital news. Other papers followed suit, including the *News & Observer* in Raleigh, North Carolina. Its pioneering website, called NandO, was the first professional digital news site.

By the early 1990s, the major newspaper publishers had recovered from the failures of earlier experiments. Major newspapers began providing their articles through services like America Online, where paying customers used dial-up modems to access various kinds of information. Such services were easier to use than the Viewtron or even a BBS, but they still did not bring publishing directly to readers in the same way newspapers did. That would require two major technological leaps.

The Birth of the Web

The first big breakthrough was the work of a computer scientist named Tim Berners-Lee. In the late 1980s,

Berners-Lee invented a way to link the networks of computers that the engineers at ARPA built in the 1960s. That became the internet when the government-run system was opened to the public in 1972. Today, the internet consists of billions of devices, from giant mainframe computers to desktops, laptops, tablets, and smartphones.

A key fact about the internet that would shape its role in journalism is that no single entity owns it—no business, no government, no multinational institution. The internet is free. Apart from standards for hardware and software and how the pieces of the internet work together, the internet is also almost entirely without rules.

Berners-Lee understood how to harness the infrastructure of the internet to share information. He invented something called hypertext markup language (HTML), enabling people to display text, images, and other material on a computer screen in whatever way they wanted. HTML shares that information across the internet by creating links that users can click on to move from one page or document to any other, anywhere in the world. The World Wide Web was born.

The invention of HTML and the web was a revolution for newspaper publishers. Suddenly, they had a tool that would allow them to deliver their content instantly and however they wanted, directly to their readers. They no longer needed services like AOL to serve as a conduit, and they could control everything about what information to present, when to do so, and how it would look.

While the web changed everything for publishers, for readers there was still another step that was needed. Berners-Lee had shown how to make web pages using

File Options Navigate Annotate

Document Title: | NASA Information Services via World Wide W

Document URL: | http://www.gsfc.nasa.gov/NASA_homepage.htm

National Aeronautics and Space Administration

National Aeronautics and
Space Administration

World Wide Web (WWW) information services

* Hot Topics * .... NASA news and subjects of public interest

NASA's Strategic Plan, Specific NASA Strategies & Policies

NASA Public Affairs

NASA Educational Programs, NASA Online Educational Resources

NASA Information Sources by Subject

NASA Centers (click on a center's name for its home page):

An early web page from NASA, displayed through Mosaic, the first widely available web browser. Mosaic and its successor, Netscape Navigator, brought the World Wide Web to millions of people.

Document Title: | NASA/Kennedy Space Center Home

Document URL: | http://www.ksc.nasa.gov/ksc.htm

NASA Kennedy Space Center Home Page

Welcome to KSC's World Wide Web (WWW) information center. From this document, you can access a variety of useful information at the Kennedy Space Center. You can find out What's New on KSC's server, or Hot Topics within NASA or Other Important Announcements.

- About Kennedy Space Center
- Facilities at KSC
- Historical Archive
- Shuttle Mission Information
- Shuttle Reference Manual
- Frequently Asked Questions
- Search for Information
- KSC Gopher server
- KSC X.500 Locator Service

Next Shuttle Mission

Back | Forward | Home | Reload | Open... | Save As... | Clone | New Window

Tim Berners-Lee

In the late 1980s, a software consultant named Tim Berners-Lee was working at a world-renowned physics laboratory outside Geneva, Switzerland, known as CERN. Scientists from all over the world would arrive at the lab, do their experiments using their own computers, then leave, taking their data with them. Those computers were incompatible with each other, and with the giant machines CERN used to run its particle accelerators.

Berners-Lee was responsible for helping the scientists work together, and he realized the best way was for computers to exchange information directly. He also realized that CERN in particular and scientists in general would benefit if their computers could communicate from wherever they were, not just when they were at the lab. That sounds obvious now, but in the late 1980s there was no easy way for computers to communicate with one another. In March 1989, Berners-Lee developed a plan for an open computer network that would extend beyond CERN. He submitted a proposal for funding to get it off the ground. That proposal would become the foundation of the World Wide Web, a term Berners-Lee coined as he was writing the code for the project in 1990.

It took Berners-Lee and his colleagues nearly two years to build a working system. They had three main innovations: hypertext transfer protocol (HTTP), which creates clickable links between documents and web pages; universal resource locators (URLs), which are electronic addresses for those documents or pages; and hypertext markup language (HTML), which allows the documents and web pages to be displayed in a web browser.

Tim Berners-Lee is the computer scientist largely responsible for the creation of the World Wide Web.

On December 25, 1990, Berners-Lee and the team at CERN created the first web page and demonstrated how such pages could be seen anywhere in the world via the internet. The World Wide Web was born. Within a few years, the initials WWW would signal a revolution in the world of human communication.

HTML, but finding those web pages and navigating between them remained difficult for the average person until 1993. That was when Marc Andreessen, a twenty-two-year-old computer science student at the University of Illinois in Urbana-Champaign, invented a web browser almost anyone could use. He named it Mosaic.

Mosaic put a graphical interface on top of the HTML-based web pages that Berners-Lee had pioneered. Without it, those pages remained a rich source of information for researchers and scholars. With it, all of the functions we take for granted today on the web became possible. A wealth of information was now easily available to million of people. The web exploded.

After launching Mosaic, Marc Andreessen went on to cofound Netscape. The company released Navigator, the first commercial web browser, in 1994. Microsoft soon launched its own browser, Internet Explorer. An era of intense competition over which browser would dominate the market had begun.

The ready availability of browsers to speed access to content on the web opened the floodgates for digital online journalism. The first online news site launched in November 1993 at the University of Florida College of Journalism and Communications. A few months later, a California newspaper, the *Palo Alto Weekly*, became the first to publish regularly on the web. Most news outlets had an online presence within a few years of those first experiments.

By the dawn of the twenty-first century, websites played a major if not dominant role in nearly all journalism in the United States, Europe, and more. Just a few years later, more Americans would be using the internet rather than reading newspapers to get their national and international news.

What Is Digital Journalism?

Here is a simple definition of digital journalism: journalism that relies on the internet to distribute content rather than publishing in newspapers or magazines or broadcasting over TV or radio. That definition hides many complex questions. Perhaps the most important is this: Who is a digital journalist?

A reporter hired by a major newspaper whose articles appear online would clearly fit the definition of a digital journalist. But what about an activist who records a protest on her cell phone and posts it to her website? Or a group of neighbors who provide information on community events and local government and also offer commentary and a place for others to do so as well?

All of these people could be considered to be practicing some form of digital journalism. Some would argue that journalism requires some degree of professional training and employment at a recognized news organization. But even the definition of a news organization, once so clearly limited to newspapers, magazines, and TV networks, has become blurred. Since it is now so easy to be connected to the internet at all times, almost everyone can be a reporter and a publisher at the same time and at little cost. When anyone can post whatever he or she likes and call it news, the problem of separating fact from fiction becomes both more difficult and more important.

Craigslist

Not that long ago, if you wanted to buy a car, sell a used television, find a job, rent an apartment, or complete any number of other commercial transactions, the first place you would look was the newspaper. There, usually in the back, were page after page of small ads placed by individuals and companies of all sizes. These were classified ads—so-called because they were grouped by category, like jobs, cars, pets, etc. Classifieds were not expensive for the buyers, but there were so many purchased that they formed the economic backbone of newspapers everywhere.

That remained the case until a man named Craig Newmark decided that the internet offered a better way of doing things. In 1995, Newmark started Craigslist, a website that offers an easy, online alternative to newspaper classified advertising pages. The site began in San Francisco and quickly spread. Local versions were launched in dozens of other cities in America and abroad.

The most important feature of Craigslist is that most of it is free. The only Craigslist ads that are not free of charge are job ads in major cities.

Craigslist cost traditional newspapers billions of dollars in advertising revenue. The effect was not limited to just classified ads, either. Newspapers also had to lower the rates they charged

Craigslist caught on quickly after it was launched. It has cost newspapers billions of dollars in lost advertising revenue.

for the much larger and more expensive display ads, while also raising the prices readers had to pay. That meant both fewer ads and fewer readers. The downward spiral for newspapers, which is still underway, had begun.

The internet makes it possible for any private individual, like this photographer documenting a 2017 protest march in Belgrade, Serbia, to perform essentially the same tasks as a professional reporter.

The Storytellers

In 1994, employees of San Francisco's two major newspapers, the *Chronicle* and the *Examiner*, went on strike to protest low wages and their management's threats to cut jobs. The strike would last only eleven days, and today few people outside of San Francisco remember much, if anything, about it. But the strike led directly to two important developments in online journalism, and the effects are still being felt today.

The first effect of the strike was almost immediate. Within hours, two separate, competing websites were born. One was run by managers from each of the two papers, and one was run by striking journalists themselves. At the time, the expertise needed to build and run a website was not widely available, even in San Francisco, just miles from the headquarters of Apple, Intel, and other computer industry giants. The journalists taught themselves the basics of HTML and set up shop in whatever space they could find.

The two news websites did not have a huge impact on either the way people produced or consumed news. Once the strike ended, the journalists went back to their desks and readers went back to their newspapers. But the ease with which the sites were created helped prove an important point: the technology of the web offered the promise of a cheaper and faster way to reach the readers of print newspapers.

The second effect of the newspaper strike was the work of one reporter who did not simply return to the way he had always done things. David Talbot was working as the Arts and Ideas editor for the *Examiner*. He had long contemplated the idea of founding a magazine, but the costs were simply too high. He was especially interested in the outcome of the website experiment that his colleagues had undertaken.

Salon

Convinced by the potential of the internet, David Talbot began looking for investors to fund a new project, an online magazine he saw as a "smart tabloid." With seed money from Apple, Talbot convinced several other *Examiner* reporters to join him at the online magazine he christened *Salon*. In November 1995, *Salon* went live. The world's first digital-only magazine had been born.

The staff of *Salon* had no examples of what an online magazine should look or feel like and no model for how to run it as a business. In the first year, according to one of *Salon*'s founders, "the media began to pay a little attention to the oddball little 'e-zine' staffed by refugees from the newspaper world." The site also

Cintra Wilson (*right*) was an early and frequent contributor to Salon.com and became a leading internet journalist through her coverage of the fashion industry.

attracted a host of writers. In many cases, *Salon* helped to launch the careers of key players in the history of internet journalism, including Andrew Sullivan, Stephanie Zacharek, and Cintra Wilson.

Salon had readers, and it had influence. As a business venture, however, it struggled. The original staff of eight grew to nearly 150, then contracted again. The company began to sell stock, and the cost of a single share rose to over fifteen dollars before crashing. (As of late 2017, shares were selling for less than ten cents apiece.) Despite these struggles, *Salon* continues to publish new reporting on politics, media, and the arts.

Matt Drudge

Salon was not the only early internet publication to make waves. Matt Drudge has been both compared to Walter Cronkite and described as a menace to honest journalism. To some, he simply makes mischief while peddling gossip. To others, he is one of the most powerful journalists in America, the leading edge of the provocative citizen reporting movement that's taking a slice of the market from traditional media giants. In short, no single individual captures the contradictions, possibilities, and pitfalls of online journalism better than Drudge.

Matt Drudge is in many ways an unlikely candidate to lead a revolution in journalism. He works alone from an apartment that could be in either Florida or California. He did not attend college and had no formal training or newspaper experience. His early career after high school consisted of jobs at a grocery store, at McDonald's, and

Matt Drudge built an email newsletter he sent to friends into the *Drudge Report*, one of the most influential websites for political commentary and news.

as a telemarketer. Then he began sending his friends an email newsletter filled with his own opinions and bits of gossip he picked up while living in Los Angeles. The email list kept growing, and Drudge moved the operation to a website in 1996.

The increased visibility did not change Drudge's basic philosophy: You don't need a college degree, editors, or fact-checkers to be a journalist. All you need is the desire to report on the news as you see it, and the means to publish the results. Drudge had the former, and the internet provided the latter.

Drudge was at best living on the fringes of the news media until January 1998. He had some sixty thousand subscribers, and tens of thousands more read his *Drudge Report* website. His readership was not insignificant but still tiny compared to the million-plus circulation of major newspapers like the *New York Times* or the *Wall Street Journal*. Drudge learned at that time that a *Newsweek* reporter, Michael Isikoff, had potentially scandalous information about Bill Clinton, who was then serving his second term as president of the United States. Yet *Newsweek*'s editors were holding the stories until more reporting could be done. Drudge beat them to the punch. On January 17, Drudge announced that *Newsweek* had information regarding an affair between the president and a young intern. The next day, Drudge revealed the name of the intern on his website: Monica Lewinsky. It was the first media mention of the name, and the massive response soon forced the story into the mainstream media. The Lewinsky scandal would haunt the Clinton presidency, ultimately leading to his impeachment in December 1998.

Drudge had helped tarnish a president, but was he practicing journalism? Many working journalists said no; he largely repackaged the work of others while adding a few bits of information he dug up himself. And he worked so fast, often updating his site multiple times each day, that there was no opportunity to screen his material for accuracy. Even beyond these questions about how he did his work, however, was the question of the content. Was it really news?

In the case of Bill Clinton, the answer was yes, as far as much of the voting public was concerned. Ever since, the readership and the influence of the *Drudge Report* has continued to grow. Drudge played an important part in helping elect George W. Bush over Al Gore in 2000 and over John Kerry in 2004, and Drudge also helped elect Donald Trump in 2016.

Arianna Huffington

In November 2004, a group of largely liberal Californians gathered at Arianna Huffington's home. They all agreed on the need for a politically liberal outlet to counter the effective and popular Matt Drudge. While Drudge had found success largely by aggregating content originally published elsewhere, Huffington and others at the party—particularly entrepreneurs Jonah Peretti and Ken Lerer—focused on taking advantage of the exploding popularity of blogging. The best way to attract people who would read and share articles, they soon decided, was to build a platform for celebrity blogging. Lerer would raise the money. Peretti would build the website. And it was up to Arianna Huffington to recruit the bloggers to the site that would bear her name: the *Huffington Post*.

Arianna Huffington launched the *Huffington Post* in 2005.

From Politics to Media

Arianna Huffington's road to building a media empire begins in Greece. Arianna Stassinopoulos was born in Athens, the daughter of a newspaper owner. For many years, that was her only connection to journalism, and it provided few clues to the role she would eventually play in changing how we get the news.

Stassinopoulos moved from Greece to England to attend Cambridge University, and she then wrote several books, including a bestseller on feminism. Next she moved to the United States and married a budding politician, Michael Huffington. She later entered politics herself with an unsuccessful run for governor of California. She continued to write books and meet people, including Hollywood and media celebrities. In 2004, she launched a blog called *AriannaOnline*.

The *Huffington Post* launched the following year, in May 2005. Its debut was inauspicious, with critics predicting it would not last long. Just one year later, *Time* included Huffington on its list of the world's one hundred most influential people. Matt Drudge made the list as well. The presidential election of 2008 catapulted the *Huffington Post* to even greater prominence. It soon had almost twice the readers of the *Drudge Report* and even surpassed such long-established outlets as the *Wall Street Journal* and the *Los Angeles Times*. By the end of 2009, the *Huffington Post* had more than ten million monthly visitors, making it one of the most heavily used sites on the internet.

In 2012, the renamed *HuffPo* (it had been purchased by AOL the previous year) became the first exclusively online

Citizen Journalists

The rise of new technologies has shifted the media landscape in fundamental ways. The power to decide what news is worth reporting once belonged solely to large media companies. But the internet—blogs, podcasts, social media sites like Facebook, streaming video, and other innovations—makes it possible for any private individual to perform essentially the same tasks as a professional reporter. The people who take on this role have come to be called citizen journalists. The phenomenon of citizen journalism offers both opportunities and risks for the way we understand current events.

Citizen journalism can take several different forms. In one form, people contribute to existing news sites run by professionals. Comments on news articles, for example, are a popular way to voice opposing viewpoints or add new information that the reporter may have missed. Before the age of online news, readers were limited to writing letters to the editors of their local newspaper. That process was slow and was limited by the amount of space the paper allotted to print letters—usually just a handful were published per issue. Today, comments on a single controversial article can continue for days or weeks.

Another form of citizen journalism is fully independent of professional news websites. There are thousands of blogs through which individuals with no formal journalism training can report on local events or express their opinions on national or world news. In remote or dangerous areas, like war zones, such blogs can become essential sources of information that would otherwise be unavailable.

news site to win a Pulitzer Prize for national reporting. The award recognized a ten-part series that the *Huffington Post*'s military correspondent, David Wood, wrote on the plight of wounded veterans.

The line between online and print newspapers blurred even further, and *HuffPo* continued to expand its staff to develop new stories. At the same time, *HuffPo* was also bringing other changes in journalism that may be more problematic. *HuffPo* has mastered the technique of repackaging content from elsewhere and driving readers to it by ensuring that *HuffPo* content always shows up high on the list of search engine results. This process, called "search engine optimization," brings in advertising dollars. To be profitable, many of *HuffPo*'s competitors must focus more on aggregating content than on developing new content themselves, which is vastly more expensive. So while *HuffPo* is a pioneer in a new kind of online journalism, it is also part of a trend that is making it ever more difficult for newsgathering operations to be viable, moneymaking businesses.

Google

Gathering, editing, and delivering the news from around the world has always been expensive. So expensive, in fact, that hardly any newspaper could actually make money just by printing the news. They traditionally made money because of what they delivered alongside the news—that is, ads. You can think of the newspaper delivered to the front door as a vehicle for getting people to look at various kinds of ads, from the classifieds to big ads for cars or airlines.

That business model worked well for a long time. By the mid-1990s, however, it was showing signs of strain. Once both readers and advertisers had easy access to cheaper or free alternatives on the web, that model began to break down. Fewer readers made newspapers less attractive to advertisers. Fewer ads meant the papers lost money and had to cut back on reporting staff, which meant readers had less content to choose from. A downward spiral was inevitable.

Perhaps no single company is more closely tied to all of these trends in journalism than Google, the world's most used internet search engine. In 1998, Sergey Brin and Larry Page, then graduate students at Stanford University, built Google. In doing so, they transformed the way we find information online. It is a complicated system, but in simple terms Google's breakthrough idea was this: you can measure the importance of any given page on the web by how many other pages have links to it. A link is a kind of seal of approval, so a page with many such links is likely to be useful and trusted. Google sorts the results of any search according to a mathematical process named for Larry Page called PageRank.

Today, Google handles billions of search requests every day, about 70 percent of the search engine traffic on the web. The word "google" itself has become a verb, meaning to search the web. As of 2017, the company was worth $600 billion, making it one of the most valuable companies in the world.

Google's secret lies in the fact that it is free and easy to use. The PageRank algorithm directs users to the information they want in seconds and brings the massive amount of information available on the web

Founded in 1998, Google has transformed the way we find information online.

down to a personal scale. With Google at their fingertips, people who once relied on newspapers to deliver them a bundle of stories on politics, weather, sports, business, movies, and so on could now pick and choose what they wanted, from any number of outlets. At the same time, newspapers had relied on having all those different sections together in one publication so they could sell advertising space they knew would reach particular audiences. With the creation of Google, yet another key part of the news business had been stripped away. The money newspapers used to pay the costs of supporting far-flung reporters began to dry up.

Wikipedia

Like Sergey Brin and Larry Page, other entrepreneurs were inspired by the quantity of information on the internet. The founders of Wikipedia, Jimmy Wales and Larry Sanger, saw that data, took a very old idea, and reinvented it for the digital age.

The act of compiling the world's knowledge into an encyclopedia, a single, authoritative reference work, has a long history. Encyclopedias took on their modern form—with in-depth articles by experts on a range of topics presented in a systematic way—in the eighteenth century.

The model for creating them became firmly established: the most respected scholars would draw up a list of the most important facts and historical events and then write the entries in a painstaking process. That process involved reviews by other experts to ensure the entries met a high standard of accuracy.

As with the practice of journalism, commerce, and much else, the birth of the internet and the web completely upended that model. The result has been a shift not only in what is considered important and worth learning about in depth, but also who is qualified to be an expert. Not that long ago, experts had advanced academic degrees from leading universities. Today, literally anyone, anywhere can contribute to the exploding body of knowledge that is available at the touch of a button or the swipe of a finger.

This part of the internet revolution occurred in 2001. Jimmy Wales, who had worked in finance before becoming an internet entrepreneur, and Larry Sanger, who had just completed a doctoral degree in philosophy, had launched a free, online encyclopedia called Nupedia in 1999. Like its printed predecessors, Nupedia relied on expert writers and editors and had a long approval process for its articles. Also like the printed versions, it moved slowly. In its first year, only twenty-one articles appeared on Nupedia.

Frustrated with the slow pace, Wales and Sanger created a second site that would allow anyone to start or modify an entry, hoping in this way to rapidly build up a collection of articles that would feed into the Nupedia review pipeline. They called the new site Wikipedia, and it launched on January 15, 2001. The idea of a website that any number of people could manage collaboratively had been around since the mid-1990s and had been dubbed a "wiki"—from the Hawaiian word for "quick." Wikipedia adopted the motto "the encyclopedia that anyone can edit," and it soon became the most heavily used wiki in the world.

By the end of its first year, Wikipedia had more than 20,000 articles in eighteen languages. Today, the English version has more than 4.5 million entries. There are more than 23 million entries in 286 other languages. The ambitious goal of Wikipedia, to "compile the sum of all human knowledge," feels within reach.

A huge army of volunteers carries out the vast majority of the work on Wikipedia. Wikipedia is the most visible and arguably the most successful example of what has become known as "crowdsourcing." Crowdsourcing is taking a function once performed by employees of a given company and instead having that task performed by an undefined but usually large network of people.

Internet entrepreneur Jimmy Wales created Wikipedia in 2001. Today, the English version has more than 4.5 million entries.

Wikipedia plays an important role in news coverage as well. New Wikipedia articles on breaking news stories can appear within hours of the events themselves and are updated constantly and in real time. In December 2004, Wikipedia even launched an offshoot called Wikinews that was intended to provide a space for collaborative journalism. (While the site still exists, it receives far fewer contributions than does Wikipedia, even for current events.)

In 2017, Wikipedia cofounder Jimmy Wales moved more directly into the news business when he launched another journalism venture called WikiTribune. His idea is to hire a team of reporters to work side by side with volunteer contributors to cover the news. Instead of paying for the site through ads, readers would pay for subscriptions or make donations, just as many make donations to support Wikipedia. Wikipedia and WikiTribune are not connected, but they spring from the same idea: communities of people can be trusted to create and maintain collections of timely, accurate information.

In a video announcing the launch of WikiTribune, Wales says that he began the new venture because "the news is broken, but we figured out how to fix it." A key part of what is broken, Wales says, is the way news websites make their money. Most news sites are supported by ads, so they engage in stiff competition to attract visitors. That competition requires a nearly constant turnover of the most eye-catching content possible. This strategy does not always lend itself to high-quality journalism. The problem is made worse by the fact that fewer and fewer people will pay to support journalism. Most people prefer to get their news from Facebook or other social media. These services show their users things they know the users will like, not things that have been proven to be true. WikiTribune is an experiment in changing the process of gathering and delivering the news.

WikiLeaks

Wikipedia quickly became the place to start researching almost any topic, though the quality of the information available there varies considerably. In 2006, an Australian computer programmer named Julian Assange launched another website, also with the word "wiki" in its name but unrelated to Wikipedia. Assange's site brought another dramatic change to the business of news and information. He called his site WikiLeaks.

In journalism, a "leak" is the unauthorized release of confidential information to the news media. Leaks occur when someone working for a government agency, a corporation, or some other organization has access to important or interesting information that is not available to the public. That individual contacts a reporter, who either releases the information or uses it as the basis for an investigation.

Leaks have long been critical to investigative journalism. Perhaps the most famous leak involved a study of the Vietnam War called the Pentagon Papers. That study, which found many troubling facts about the way the war was being carried out, was secret until an employee of the company that conducted it gave the study to the *New York Times*. The government sued the paper to prevent it from publishing the story, a case that went all the way to the Supreme Court. The government's suit resulted in one of the most important court decisions about freedom of the press, *New York Times Co. v. United States.*

For nearly the entire history of journalism, a leak involved a relationship between a reporter and his or her source for the information. WikiLeaks changed that. The site enables anonymous sources and leakers to make original documents available worldwide. In its early days, WikiLeaks functioned much like Wikipedia. Anyone could submit and edit material that was made public almost instantly. Beginning in 2010, however, WikiLeaks began to take a very different approach. In November of that year, WikiLeaks said it had received more than 250,000 diplomatic cables about the wars in Iraq and Afghanistan. These cables were acquired from an anonymous source later revealed to be US Army intelligence analyst Chelsea Manning. Rather than release all the documents directly to the public, WikiLeaks chose to give portions of the collection to four European newspapers. One shared its collection with the *New York Times.* According to Assange, WikiLeaks was relying on the news organizations to determine which parts of the documents were newsworthy and should be released, and which were too sensitive and should remain secret.

The idea that a source of information can work for multiple newspapers at the same time, and potentially could stop cooperating if a paper behaves in a way the source does not like, is something very new for journalists. It has the potential to change the way stories about sensitive material are produced. The broad and public release of classified information also means that governments might take a more aggressive approach to stopping leaks.

In 2006, Australian computer programmer Julian Assange created WikiLeaks, a website that enables anonymous sources and leakers to make original documents available wordwide.

WikiLeaks raises the question of who is a journalist. Julian Assange claims that he is one. The US Department of State says he is not a journalist and is instead a "political actor." Some members of Columbia University's School of Journalism, among the most prominent in the country, wrote a letter in 2010 to President Barack Obama in support of Assange. By publishing the diplomatic cables, they said, "WikiLeaks is engaging in journalistic activity protected by the First Amendment." They argued that "as a historical matter, government overreaction to publication of leaked material in the press has always been more damaging to American democracy then the leaks themselves."

Podcasts

In 2001, Apple released a new portable device that most people would use to play their favorite songs. They called it the iPod. But the iPod was not limited to music. Anything that could be recorded could be put into an audio file and played while on the go. People began experimenting with the new format, recording shows on a variety of topics that listeners could download. Combining the idea of traditional radio broadcast with the new way of delivering the content, the format was named the "podcast."

Podcasts were not terribly popular at first. The early podcasts were often amateur productions. They also faced stiff competition from other new media. Another problem was that it was hard to sell advertising on podcasts. The technology at the time made it hard to say for sure how many people listened to any given podcast, and thus heard any given ad.

That began to change in 2014. That year, the podcast *Serial* grabbed international attention and reached five million downloads faster than any podcast ever. The percentage of Americans listening to podcasts doubled between 2008 and 2015. Over a third of Americans now say they have listened to a podcast. Major news organizations like the *Financial Times* and the *New York Times* launched their own podcasts. New ways of tracking ads on podcasts have helped boost the money pouring into producing new shows. By 2016, the podcast business had come of age.

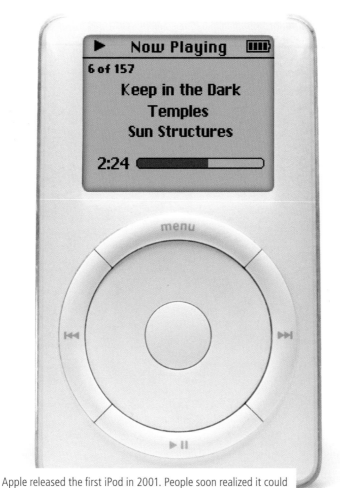

Apple released the first iPod in 2001. People soon realized it could be used to play any kind of audio, and the podcast was born.

Social media played a key role in the protests across the Middle East—like this one in Cairo's Tahrir Square—that became known as the Arab Spring.

Breaking Stories That Changed Journalism

April 19, 1995, marks a key turning point for several elements of the story of contemporary journalism: how we get urgent news and how reliable we believe it to be. In the early hours of that Wednesday morning, a rented truck, packed with some 4,800 pounds (2,177 kilograms) of explosives, rolled to a stop in front of the Alfred P. Murrah Building in Oklahoma City. The Murrah Building housed the offices of six separate federal government agencies, United States Army and Marine recruiting offices, and a daycare facility. At 9:02 a.m., the truck bomb exploded. It nearly tore the nine-story building in half and killed 168 people, including 19 children. At the time, it was the worst terrorist attack in American history.

Today, detailed pictures and accounts of an incident like the Oklahoma City bombing would be available worldwide instantly. In 1995, however, the use of the web to provide coverage of breaking news was in its infancy. News websites were for the most part limited

The bombing of the Alfred P. Murrah Building in Oklahoma City, Oklahoma, in 1995 was one of the first events to show the potential of the internet for covering breaking news.

to circulating stories that were originally published elsewhere, usually in print. Only one cable TV station, CNN, offered twenty-four-hour news coverage.

The potential of the internet was already evident to people working in the news industry. Sadly, it took a tragedy on the scale of the Oklahoma City bombing to turn that potential into reality. Within minutes of the news breaking about the bombing and its terrible aftermath, editors and journalists at online news services began frantically posting whatever information they could lay their hands on. This included maps of Oklahoma City, eyewitness accounts, details of relief efforts, lists of survivors and the hospitals treating them, and more.

The public realization that the most up-to-date information on the bombing could be found online spread just as quickly. Key news sites ground to a halt under the onslaught of users. The capacity of the web to provide a reliable source of news clearly needed to expand. Nevertheless, Oklahoma City provided compelling evidence that the internet was now an integral part of the way people got their information, particularly regarding breaking and dramatic stories.

The bombing also revealed the darker side of reporting breaking news. Those behind the bombing were unknown in the first hours and days. Many news outlets, including CBS, ABC, and CNN, reported the suspicion that Middle Eastern terrorists were responsible. "A US government source has told CBS News that it has Middle East terrorism written all over it," said the *CBS Evening News*. "It has every single earmark of the Islamic car-bombers of the Middle East," wrote one syndicated columnist in the *Chicago Tribune*. In the *New York Times*,

Timothy McVeigh was arrested just ninety minutes after the bombing, despite early reports that foreign terrorists were responsible. He was tried along with two other men and convicted in 1997.

another wrote: "Whatever we are doing to destroy Mideast terrorism, the chief terrorist threat against Americans, has not been working."

The focus on Middle Eastern terrorism proved to be misplaced. Just ninety minutes after the bomb exploded, a US-born army veteran named Timothy McVeigh was stopped by an Oklahoma highway patrolman for driving a car without a license plate. The police officer found guns in the car, and McVeigh was arrested. Forensic evidence quickly linked him and two other men, Terry Nichols and Michael Fortier, to the bombing. The three men were tried and convicted in 1997. McVeigh was executed in 2001.

Despite the rapid arrest and conviction of the bombers, the internet would prove fertile ground for conspiracy theories about who was behind the tragedy in Oklahoma City. Those unfounded theories persist to this day and have been blamed for the drop in trust of both media and government.

The Internet Bubble Bursts

Throughout the 1990s, more and more newspapers, broadcast TV stations, and cable companies began to take advantage of new computer technology. The technology changed the way they did business, but not in radical or fundamental ways. The web added a new facet to what they did, a new way to get their product to the people who wanted it.

Newspaper reporters still worked their sources and wrote their stories, editors edited them, and they ended up in print. The new feature was that these articles were available online as well. Television and cable companies took what they did best—covering breaking new stories—and brought that to the web as well. Information still ran in one direction: from the reporters to the consumers, through the filter of editors or producers.

On January 22, 1996, the *New York Times* went digital for the first time. According to the paper's own coverage of the event, the online edition offered "readers around the world immediate access to most of the daily newspaper's contents." The electronic newspaper was "part of a strategy to extend the readership of The Times and to create opportunities for the company in the electronic media industry."

Other major papers and news services quickly followed suit: the *Chicago Tribune*, the Associated Press, the *Wall Street Journal*, and others went online. But the big newspapers and media giants were still reluctant to exploit the revolutionary potential of the web. They had good reasons to join the web frenzy. Money was pouring in as more and more companies rushed to advertise their

The *New York Times* produced its first digital edition in January 1996. Other major newspapers quickly followed suit.

goods and services online. The problem was that because internet ads were so cheap compared to old-fashioned print ads, they actually did not produce much revenue for the companies selling them. They would have to sell many more online ads to have a real impact on the profits of the company.

That issue would remain hidden because, in the late 1990s, new companies were being born every day that did not and would not ever turn a profit. Yet these very companies were considered to be worth many millions of dollars. They sold stock and created vast wealth for their founders, employees, and investors, at least for a time. They created what came to called the "dot-com bubble."

The most dramatic example came in January 2000. America Online (AOL), one of the dominant companies of the early web era, bought the long-established media giant Time Warner. Time Warner owned *Time* magazine, CNN, and HBO, among other renowned brands. The idea that an upstart web-based company was now in charge of some of the most important media outlets in the country seemed monumental. It was thought to be the harbinger of things to come, the birth of a new industry. That would turn out to be true, but not in the way anyone expected.

AOL bought Time Warner for nearly $100 billion more than it was worth. Most experts now agree that it was one of the worst mistakes in American business history. The deal would prove to be the turning point for the dot-com bubble. Within a year, stock prices for dozens of technology companies collapsed. Even big newspapers like the *New York Times* saw their revenues from online advertising disappear. The web did not go away. In fact, more and more people were using it. But now journalists would have to find even more innovative ways to reach them.

9/11 Attacks

The terrorist attacks of September 11, 2001, caused unprecedented demand for instant access to the news. The aftermath of the tragedies brought about significant changes in the way people gather information and what kinds of information they have available.

The impact that the terrorist attacks would have on journalism took two different forms. One was the immediate aftermath of the events themselves, when the gap between the potential for the internet to provide

The aftermath of the terrorist attacks of September 11, 2001, brought about significant changes in the way people gather information and what kinds of information are available.

news and the current state of the technology became clear. The other would take far longer to emerge.

When the news of the attacks broke, traffic to high-profile news websites spiked dramatically. In fact, more people tried to visit those sites than ever before. Traffic increased a thousandfold. There were more than nine million requests every hour for CNN's main web page. Websites for major papers and television networks crashed. People who had gone first to the internet moved to more traditional outlets like television and radio. Even Google directed people away from the web. Google users on 9/11 found this message:

> If you are looking for news, you will find the most current information on TV or radio. Many online news services are not available, because of extremely high demand. Below are links to news

sites, including cached copies as they appeared earlier today.

The initial inability of news websites to handle the demand revealed that they were not quite ready to serve as the primary source of breaking news for millions of people. According to Nick Wrenn, an editor for CNN.com in Europe: "Like all the other major news providers, we fell over for a while. CNN.com had ramped up its servers ahead of the US election [the previous year] but it wasn't enough. The site was temporarily stripped back to a low-graphic story so we could give people the latest headlines."

Despite the initial failure of major news websites to handle the surge of demand, the unique strengths of the internet as a source for news became clear almost as quickly. In particular, the 9/11 attacks highlighted the ability of the web to offer images and information from multiple perspectives through blog posts, personal web pages, comments, and discussion forums.

Many non-news sites became important sources of information and commentary about 9/11. Among the most compelling were stories from people who had either seen the World Trade Center collapse or had firsthand knowledge of the events in New York, Washington, and Pennsylvania. Pamela LiCalzi O'Connell, a technology reporter for the *New York Times*, wrote about the phenomenon a little more than a week after the attacks:

Many New Yorkers wrote online about what they experienced escaping from downtown Manhattan or watching the destruction of the towers. These stories, more numerous than could ever fit into this or any newspaper, appeared on personal Web pages and discussion boards and were forwarded by e-mail to millions. By early this week, directories and other centralized listings of survivor stories and firsthand accounts began to appear—social history in its rawest, tear-stained form.

The Virginia Tech Shooting

On April 16, 2007, a gunman named Seung-Hui Cho killed thirty-two students and faculty members before killing himself on the campus of Virginia Polytechnic Institute and State University, in Blacksburg, Virginia. The massacre came just eight months after Facebook had opened its virtual doors to the world beyond college campuses. Facebook and other online resources, particularly blogs, would play central roles in the way information—and misinformation—about the events at Virginia Tech was spread worldwide.

Traffic to Facebook increased fivefold in the space of twenty-four hours after the shootings. Students who were told to remain in their dorms turned to Facebook to check on friends, share news, and talk about their experiences. Newspaper and TV reporters covering the story also created Facebook accounts to find eyewitnesses or people touched by the shootings. Those sites, however, sometimes spread misinformation. As a result, the wrong person was at first identified as the shooter. That mistake was broadcast on national television.

Several different kinds of blogs also shaped coverage of the shootings. Both the *Collegiate Times*—Virginia

Tech's student newspaper—and the *Roanoke Times* used a blog to keep readers informed of breaking news. New information was posted fast, sometimes minute-by-minute, like these updates from the *Roanoke Times*:

1:06 p.m.

Virginia Tech campus is quiet, with few students walking about. Most buildings are evacuated and police are telling people to leave and not come back today. Dormitories are locked down.

A heavy police presence is evident, with armed officers visible all around the Drillfield.

Freshman Hector Takahashi said he'd been in a class in Pamplin Hall, near Norris Hall, around 9:30 a.m. Students were talking about a shooting in West Ambler Johnston.

"Then all of a sudden, we were like, 'Whoa—were those shots?'" he said. There were two quick bangs, then a pause, then a fusillade of at least 30 shots, he said.

1:05 p.m.

Multiple people in the Virginia Tech athletic department have said all players have been accounted for on the football, men's basketball, women's basketball, softball, golf and men's tennis teams. Reporters are trying to contact coaches of the other teams.

The next scheduled on-campus athletic event is a baseball game Wednesday against William and Mary.

Blacksburg town offices are closed for the day.

Many bloggers who were not journalists but who were on campus that day also became part of the news coverage, posting their thoughts and observations on many different blogging websites. One blogger named Bryce Carter, writing under the name ntcoolfool, received international attention and had mainstream media producers requesting help finding cell phone videos after he posted a video clip of police cars heading to the scene of the massacre. He wrote one of the first posts about the shootings:

> My friends and I got out of class at about 9:50. Walked across campus. The wind blew with flurries about. Sirens were in the distance and I saw an undercover cop car go about 80 down one of the drives. That was odd. In front one of the dorms, West AJ, were several police cars, lights off and parked. We started talking about how there are always situations that cops rush across campus for and we never hear about.
>
> Then several people walked by and told us there was a shooting and campus was closed. No one is allowed to cross the drillfield. Hmm. We went ahead to eat some food as cops were stationed in front, checking ID for everyone. I walked with my friend to his dorm to get his stuff as an omniscient announcement echoed across campus:
>
> "This is an emergency. This is an emergency. Take shelter in doors immediately. Stay away from windows and remain inside."

Mainstream media outlets also turned to blogs to find eyewitnesses and student testimonials. After Virginia Tech, the line between journalists and non-journalists began to blur.

Facebook and blogs would play central roles in the way information was spread worldwide about the 2007 massacre of thirty-two students and faculty members at Virginia Tech.

Blogger

By the late 1990s, some early adopters of the internet were using personal websites to publish their opinions or simply accounts of their daily lives. They went by various names, including "diarist" and "journaler." In 1995, a computer programmer named Jorn Barger launched a website he called Robot Wisdom, which included daily links reflecting his interests. The site offered a "day-to-day log of his reading and intellectual pursuits." In 1997, Barger coined the term "WebLog" to describe this unique form of publishing on the web. The term was shortened to "blog" shortly thereafter.

The format did not catch on at first because users still needed sophisticated programming skills. That changed in 1999. The software company Pyra released a program it called Blogger, which made it simple to set up and constantly update

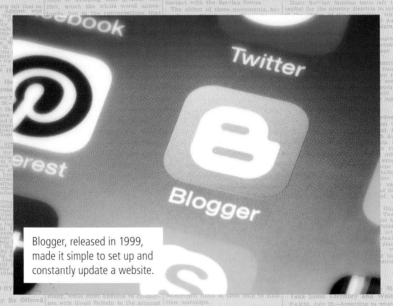

Blogger, released in 1999, made it simple to set up and constantly update a website.

a website. Blogger enabled anyone to easily create a web page or to post content without needing to know how to write HTML code.

Blogging took off. Within just a few years, several thousand weblogs were being launched every day. Less than a decade after the debut of Blogger, the number of weblogs was estimated to be well over one hundred million.

Today, some journalists who work for conventional media outlets also have their own blogs, and there are blogs that consist of links to mainstream news sources, but most blogging is too narrow or biased to qualify as journalism. On the other hand, blogs can point reporters to stories they might otherwise miss. Blogs can also serve an important role of pointing out sloppy or erroneous reporting.

The Arab Spring

Just as the Virginia Tech shooting realized the internet's potential for citizen journalism, the Arab Spring showed social media's ability to galvanize thousands for political change.

The rural Tunisian town of Sidi Bouzid sits about 170 miles (274 km) south of the capital, Tunis. It was the home of a twenty-six-year-old street vendor named Mohamed Bouazizi. Bouazizi supported his six siblings and his mother with his meager earnings, even though he did not have a vendor's permit. In December 2010, Bouazizi was setting up his wooden cart to sell fruits and vegetables. The police asked for his permit and then demanded he hand over his cart. Bouazizi refused. In despair, he walked to a government building and set himself on fire.

Bouazizi's protest sparked a movement. People took to the street in Sidi Bouzid that same day. When images of those protests, captured by cell phone cameras, were shared on the internet, other protests broke out across the country. Within days, Tunisia's longtime president, Zine al-Abidine Ben Ali, resigned from office. The Tunisian Revolution led to revolts that toppled regimes in Libya and Egypt and to civil war or sustained street demonstrations against the governments in more than a dozen other countries.

The uprisings across the Middle East became known as the Arab Spring. Social media would play a central role in shaping how the rest of the world came to understand the rapidly unfolding events. Some observers also argued that internet platforms like Twitter and Facebook were crucial to organizing and spreading the protests. However, it is more likely that the greater impact of social media was to inform people outside of the region rather than motivate protest from those living in places like Egypt and Yemen. (Relatively few of the protesters had reliable access to the internet.)

Both newspapers and television stations relied on participants in the protests to bring unique and unfiltered content to international audiences. Some of the most dramatic coverage of events in Egypt, for example, came during the occupation of Tahrir Square, a major public gathering space in Cairo. Protesters had taken to the street to demand the ouster of President Hosni Mubarak. A small sample of the tweets from Tahrir Square from a single day in February 2011 (captured by the *Guardian*) offers a sense of how the events were documented in real time through social media:

- @TravellerW: And a lovely revolution to you too, sir. Live from Cairo – we are back and excited like we've never been before! #Egypt #jan25
- @tarekshalaby: Internet's back in #Egypt. I've been camping out in Tahrir for 4 days n will remain until #Mubarak leaves. #jan25
- @3arabawy: Here r the latest updates: The govt is countermobilizing against us now. There r several pro-Mubarak protests taking place in Cairo now.
- @norashalaby: Down w Mubarak graffiti that was all over city now being changed by pro-Mubarak thugs #Jan25

- @Sandmonkey: The mood in Egypt today is different. Too many people still beholden to the mentality of slaves. This is so frustrating. #jan25
- @3arabawy: We r at very critical stage. The counterrevolution is out in full steam. You will collect our dead bodies from garbage bins if we don't win.
- @Sandmonkey: A lot of people talking on the street, saying that this is good enough, & we shouldn't forget what Mubarak did for us. The Irony baffles me.

New media like YouTube, Facebook, and Twitter became the pipelines to more traditional media outlets. Television stations, in particular, turned to videos uploaded from cell phones rather than relying on their own correspondents. Some of these videos would be viewed millions of times. Reporters also used Twitter and Facebook to identify activists to interview, and some became international media stars. The ability of social media to magnify stories and individuals has only grown since the Arab Spring began.

Serial

The reporting on 9/11, the Virginia Tech massacre, and the Arab Spring shows just how difficult it is to classify journalists in the digital age. Many people lie somewhere between professional journalists and everyday citizens as they record events and relay firsthand accounts. The *Serial* podcast adds another wrinkle to how we classify reporting. Was *Serial* host Sarah Koenig a journalist or a detective?

The technology for producing and distributing podcasts has been available since 2004. But it took ten years for the format to really take hold and become an important part of the landscape of online journalism. Podcasts are now everywhere, and their exploding popularity can be traced almost entirely to Koenig's show, which debuted on October 3, 2014.

Serial explored a single story, recounting as it happened an investigation into a murder that occurred in Baltimore County, Maryland, in 1999. The show combined elements of journalism with those of drama, including cliffhangers and mysteries. Since it unfolded almost in real time, and neither the reporters nor the listeners knew exactly how the next episode would turn out, it became irresistible for millions of people. Less than one year after its launch, *Serial* had been downloaded nearly seventy million times.

The story behind *Serial* revolves around Hae Min Lee, a high school senior who disappeared in January 1999. Her body was found six weeks later; she had been strangled. Her boyfriend, Adnan Syed, was convicted of the murder based for the most part on testimony of a friend who claimed that Syed had killed Lee, and that he had helped bury her body. The friend's story changed a few times. Furthermore, police could find no physical evidence linking Syed to the crime, but a jury was nevertheless convinced of Syed's guilt. Syed, who was seventeen years old at the time of the crime, was sentenced to life in prison.

Another friend of Syed's believed that he was innocent and that his attorney mishandled the case. In 2013, she contacted a journalist, Sarah Koenig, who worked as a producer for the National Public Radio show *This American*

Political Cartoons Go Digital

A political cartoon by award-winning editorial cartoonist Matt Wuerker

As print newspapers have struggled with declining budgets, one casualty has been the political cartoon. Once a standard feature of every major paper, the number of editorial cartoonists has steadily declined over the past fifty years. But while the rise of the internet has largely been to blame for the trend, technology may also offer new opportunities.

The most obvious strength of the internet for a political cartoonist is distribution. Whereas it was once the case that the highest compliment you could pay a cartoonist was to clip his or her work from the paper and post it on an office door or a refrigerator, today cartoons can circulate worldwide with the click of a mouse. That can vastly magnify the impact a cartoon can have. Many political cartoons have "gone viral," or been shared thousands or even millions of times across various social media platforms. A single cartoon seen that many times can shape the way people view an issue or a public figure.

The internet also makes new kinds of cartooning possible. In 2012, Matt Wuerker of *Politico* won the Pulitzer Prize for Editorial Cartooning, the first time the award was given to a cartoonist for a largely online publication. Wuerker's cartoons range from traditional to more innovative formats, such as games and animations. Other papers have followed that lead. The *Los Angeles Times* created a political blog—a blend of commentary and cartoon—called *Top of the Ticket* that is only available online. Along the same lines, the animated cartoons on Washingtonpost.com also provide commentary on major news issues and political developments.

Life. Koenig's effort to discover what actually happened between Adnan Syed and Hae Min Lee became *Serial.*

At the beginning of episode 1, Koenig says, "For the last year, I've spent every working day trying to figure out where a high-school kid was for an hour after

Podcasts are now a major part of the media landscape, due in large part to the work of journalist Sarah Koenig on her 2014 podcast, *Serial.*

school one day in 1999." She is not a "detective, or a private investigator, or even a crime reporter." Koenig's willingness to take her listeners along as she dives into the story provided a unique opportunity to understand how reporters do their jobs. She details, for example, her efforts to track down the family of the victim in Korea:

> In my twenty-plus years of reporting, I've never tried as hard to find anyone. Letters in English and in Korean, phone calls, social media, friends of friends of friends, two private detectives, Korean-speaking researchers, people knocking on doors in three different states, calls to South Korea. We never heard back from them. I learned a few days ago that they know what we're doing; my best guess is they want no part of it, which I respect.

Koenig set a high standard for journalistic diligence—calling everyone involved, assessing all the facts, and examining her own potential biases. The effect was both compelling and believable, so much so that the court took a new look at the case. In June 2016, a Baltimore court overturned Syed's conviction and ordered a new trial. However, not all podcasts have shown the same commitment to accurate reporting. The spread of podcasts provides yet another powerful tool that can be used either to entertain and inform or to spread false or misleading information.

President Donald Trump used the phrase "fake news" on Twitter soon after he was elected, and it quickly became a popular shorthand way to describe any sensational story that may or may not be the result of political bias.

Online Journalism and the Problem of Fake News

The phrase "fake news" became an unavoidable part of any discussion of print and television journalism in early 2017. Donald Trump began to use the phrase on Twitter, first as president-elect and then as president, and it quickly became a popular shorthand way to describe any sensational story that may or may not be the result of political bias. But the idea, and the phrase itself, has a much longer history.

People seeking political or financial gain have always been willing to disseminate lies or misleading information. As far back as the eighth century, early supporters of the Catholic Church circulated a bogus document claiming that Emperor Constantine of Rome had turned over most of his empire to the pope.

The period in United States history that most closely resembles what we see on the internet today was the late nineteenth century. That was the era that became famous for what came to be called yellow journalism.

The source for the term yellow journalism is uncertain but most likely stems from a popular cartoon of the era, the Yellow Kid. The cartoon, featuring a bucktoothed street urchin always dressed in an oversized yellow nightshirt, was the creation of cartoonist Richard Outcault. The strip began in the *New York World* and was a huge hit, spawning playing cards, dolls, and even cigarettes featuring the Yellow Kid. In 1896, the rival the *New York Journal* offered Outcault a huge salary to leave the *World*. He did, so the *World* hired a different artist to draw a new Yellow Kid cartoon. Now there were two Yellow Kids, and the papers became known as the Yellow Kid papers, and then simply the yellow papers. Their style of covering the news became known as yellow journalism.

The Yellow Kid cartoons themselves did little to peddle stories that were dubious or outright false. The *World* and the *Journal*, on the other hand, because infamous for doing just that in their articles. The contest over the cartoon was part of a much larger rivalry between the owners of the two papers. They were the giants of American journalism: Joseph Pulitzer owned the *World*, and William Randolph Hearst owned the *Journal.* Pulitzer and Hearst began a fierce battle to increase the circulation of their papers, each trying to come up with the most sensational and salacious stories.

The battle reached its peak in the late 1890s, during the lead-up to the Spanish-American War. Cuba

E YELLOW KID'S R-R-R-REVENGE; Or, How the Painter's Son Got Fresh.

The Yellow Kid cartoons did not spread false or dubious stories, but the newspapers that ran the comic strip became infamous for that practice, which came to be known as "yellow journalism."

was a Spanish colony at the time, and as its fight for independence gathered steam, many people in the United States called upon Spain to withdraw. Hearst and Pulitzer devoted more and more attention to the tensions in Cuba, fighting to sell more and more papers with bold headlines and creative reporting. They printed stories that were often inaccurate and sometimes false.

The issue came to a head on February 15, 1898. An American warship, the USS *Maine*, exploded and sank in Havana Harbor. Observers on the scene at the time said the explosion had come from inside the ship, but the *World* and the *Journal* published unfounded rumors of plots to sink it. When an investigation later stated that the explosion had come from a mine in the harbor, the papers seized upon it and called for war. The phrase "Remember the *Maine!*" became a rallying cry. The Spanish-American War began later that year.

Fake News as Satire

For much of the time since the Spanish-American War, the term "fake news" meant a deliberate hoax created by publishers in order to sell more papers. There are hundreds of examples of newspaper hoaxes from even before the era of yellow journalism to today, on topics ranging from strange pets to mermaids to men on the moon. A glance at the tabloids in the local grocery store demonstrates that the desire to sell papers based on the most outrageous stories imaginable is alive and well.

Most mainstream newspapers and working journalists began to see themselves in a different light by the early years of the twentieth century. Readers began to expect that the press would provide relevant and accurate accounts of local and world events and would be vigilant to prevent misleading or false stories from becoming part of the national conversation. Fake news still existed, but it was the province of entertainers and comedians who used real events as the starting point for satire.

In 1975, comedian Chevy Chase launched a segment on the weekly comedy revue *Saturday Night Live* called Weekend Update with the words "I'm Chevy Chase, and you're not." Weekend Update poked fun at the institution of the nightly network news broadcast, while also offering its own commentary on various elected

Jon Stewart used his platform on *The Daily Show* to relay both comedy and social commentary. For some people, it became a favored source of current information.

officials and their policies. Weekend Update has remained part of the American media culture ever since, launching the careers of many comedians who either wrote for the segment or served as its anchor. In 1994, one of those anchors, Norm MacDonald, opened his edition of Weekend Update this way: "I'm Norm MacDonald, and now the fake news."

The growth of cable television allowed the news-as-satire format to spread. In 1996, the cable station Comedy Central launched *The Daily Show*, hosted first by comedian Craig Kilborn and later, more famously, by Jon Stewart. *The Daily Show* and its spinoff, *The Colbert Report*, would become the preeminent sources for comedy based entirely on current events. Together, the two shows could be seen twenty-three times per week, providing ample opportunity to cover important events repeatedly and in depth. Over time, many people began to turn to the comedy shows instead of traditional newscasts for current information—a development that neither Stewart nor Stephen Colbert, host of the *Colbert Report*, endorsed. Many prominent newsmakers and politicians began to appear on the shows, recognizing that they reached an important audience of younger viewers. By 2005, Stewart could legitimately be introduced as "the most trusted name in fake news."

Propaganda

Intentionally misleading people in order to get a laugh or make a comment about the state of the nation seems harmless enough. There is another form of fake news that is even older and far more dangerous. It is called propaganda.

The word itself is ancient and honorable. It dates to the early seventeenth century and referred to efforts by the Catholic Church to spread the faith around the world. It was a neutral term that meant disseminating information to support a cause. The idea of using newspapers, pamphlets, and other forms of mass communication to influence popular opinion did not become entrenched for several centuries. During the Civil War, for example, American abolitionists waged a campaign against slavery using a variety of media, an effort that was a relatively early form of propaganda. (However, they did not use that term.)

Over time, the idea of propaganda began to be seen in a much more negative light. The practice in its modern form dates to the start of World War I. The British were particularly effective at using mass communication techniques to shape world opinion about the war. When World War II broke out, the Nazi government in Germany was determined not to let that happen again. The Nazis created the most far-reaching propaganda effort the world had yet seen. That effort largely shapes our contemporary understanding of propaganda as destructive to our ability to understand events: governments providing misleading or simply false information primarily to further an agenda, often by evoking an emotional rather than a rational response.

With the development of modern communications techniques, particularly online, the line between propaganda and other kinds of fake news or even straightforward efforts at persuasion has begun to blur. Propaganda has typically been associated with the efforts of governments to change public opinion, especially

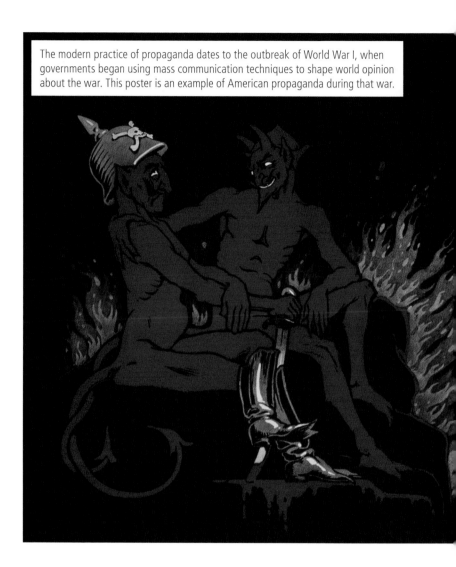

The modern practice of propaganda dates to the outbreak of World War I, when governments began using mass communication techniques to shape world opinion about the war. This poster is an example of American propaganda during that war.

during wartime. The growth of social media and other technologies, however, has made the tools of mass communication available to anyone. That makes the task of determining the source of what appears to be news far more difficult. When the source of information is unclear, it is also harder to judge whether that information is accurate and objective.

Chums

"When I really began to admire You, my friend, was when you pulled that Lusitania job. When You did that, I said to myself— 'There's a man after my own heart!'"

ON COLLIER Patriotic Series NO.2

The Source and Spread of Fake News

While fake news is an old phenomenon, its ability to spread has never been greater. In 2017, Tim Berners-Lee argued that fake news presented among the most urgent and troubling developments on the internet. The internet acts as a worldwide megaphone, taking stories that may have once found a small group of interested readers and turning them into global headlines. There are two related processes at work: the first is the creation of fake news; the second is its dissemination.

In the digital age, when anyone can be a publisher of information, anyone can also be a source of fake news. While it is true that individuals can sometimes be the source of false or misleading stories that spread, the far bigger problem is companies that create fake stories for profit. Social media platforms like Facebook and Twitter reach so many people that it was almost inevitable that unscrupulous businesses would tap into the billions of users to draw people to their own sites with sensational stories to bring in money through ads. Websites like *National Report* and *World News Daily Report* are unapologetic purveyors of hoaxes on a wide variety of topics—celebrities behaving badly, incredible new creatures, space aliens. These publications have no objective other than to make money.

There are other sources of misinformation that have the specific goals of changing public opinion about particular political figures or their policies. The content of these sites, which exist on both ends of the political spectrum, can at times come close to the standard definition of propaganda.

Consider a few examples among many from the conservative side of American politics and from the liberal side. In 2007, Andrew Breitbart, who had helped found the *Huffington Post*, created his own site for news and commentary and called it Breitbart.com. It began, like the *Drudge Report*, as a place to find links to stories from other sources but gradually developed a staff of its own to write original stories. Nearly all of those stories reflect the ideology of the far-right.

Breitbart believed that the national news media was skewed to the political left, and he created Breitbart.com to provide a right-wing alternative. He died suddenly of a heart attack in 2012, just before he was going to launch a consolidated news site, the *Breitbart News Network*. That effort was taken over by Stephen K. Bannon, a Hollywood producer who had specialized in conservative documentaries. Under Bannon, *Breitbart News* became the most widely read conservative news site in the United States.

Breitbart attracts far more visitors than any single site on the liberal side of the political spectrum. A number of left-leaning sites, among them *Media Matters for America*, *Vox*, and *ThinkProgress*, offer an exclusively liberal perspective on the news. Like Breitbart, these sites have on occasion published stories that come close to being intentionally misleading or outright false. Watchdog groups on both sides monitor news sites constantly and are quick to highlight those that they think are designed to enter the mainstream media and shape the coverage of important events, particularly in politics.

These are only a handful of the countless sources of misleading or false information available on the web. It is important to understand those sources and their biases, but it is just as important to understand how fake news spreads. The two most important platforms in this regard are Facebook and Twitter.

Fake News Gone Viral

In the United States, more than 60 percent of Americans receive news via social media. But fake news gets a much greater boost from Facebook and other similar services than real news does. Researchers at Northwestern University determined that 30 percent of all fake news traffic could be linked back to Facebook, as opposed to only 8 percent of real news traffic. One major reason for that trend is the algorithms that Facebook uses to create news feeds and compilations based on a user's preferences and browsing history. Those algorithms are powerful tools for providing people with content they are likely to be interested in reading. However, they do not screen articles for accuracy and objectivity. At the same time, traditional news media are losing advertisers to digital platforms, and thus have fewer resources to provide objective and independent reporting.

Another key complement of fake news on the internet, particularly on Twitter, is the ability of software to create thousands of phony accounts, called "bots" (short for "robots"). Twitter bots can help particular stories go viral by retweeting messages millions of times, far faster than would be the case for real Twitter users. In 2016, experts at Indiana University in Bloomington analyzed fourteen million Twitter messages. They found that bots spread fake stories far more rapidly and widely than humans. Thus, bots were key to making certain stories go viral.

To take just one example of how the process works, consider what happened in Louisiana on September 11, 2014. Residents of Saint Mary Parish began receiving notifications via Twitter about an explosion at a chemical plant nearby. Hundreds of Twitter accounts documented the disaster, with eyewitness stories, photos of flames engulfing the plant, and even video of the explosion. Journalists and media outlets across the county heard

The *Times-Picayune* Wins the Pulitzer for Public Service

Hurricane Katrina hit New Orleans in August 2005. As it neared the coast, dozens of reporters at the *New Orleans Times-Picayune*, the largest daily newspaper in the city, decided not to evacuate. They hunkered down in the newsroom. When they could not operate the presses because the power went out, they were still able to use the paper's website, Nola.com, to post updates throughout the storm and in its wake.

Reporters added new reports to the blog continuously. With no print editions available, for days Nola.com was the essential source of information about the disaster, both for residents of New Orleans and for people watching worldwide. On a typical day before the storm, there were about eight hundred thousand page views at Nola.com. Just after the storm, that exploded to more than thirty million views per day. Citizen journalists also took advantage of the website to post their own reports.

Despite the hardships and the chaos, the *Times-Picayune* continued its deep and responsible coverage. For its efforts, the paper was awarded the 2006 Pulitzer Prize for Public Service (which it shared with the *Sun Herald* in Biloxi, Mississippi.) The Pulitzer committee specifically called out the work of Nola.com, making it the first time that an online publication was recognized with journalism's highest honor. Jim Amoss, editor of the *Times-Picayune*, paid tribute to the blog's contributors when he accepted the prize, saying they "were integral to everything we published, and made us an around-the-clock vital link to readers scattered across the nation."

The *New Orleans Times-Picayune* and its website, Nola.com, won a Pulitzer Prize in 2006 for its coverage of Hurricane Katrina. It was the first time that an online publication was recognized with journalism's highest honor. Here, a photo shows the hurricane's aftermath.

about the crisis within minutes. One Twitter account showed a screenshot of CNN's home page as evidence that the explosion was an important national story. Another showed that the terrorist organization ISIS had claimed credit for blowing up the plant, on the anniversary of the most famous of all terrorist attacks.

This was all frightening, newsworthy, and completely fake. Within hours, the managers of the plant had put out a message saying there had been no explosion. But this was no simple hoax. It was a sophisticated and well-planned effort involving a team of computer programmers and editors. Then an army of automated bots spread their creations worldwide. According to an investigative report in the *New York Times*, the chemical plant hoax, along with other hoaxes from about the same time—false stories about an Ebola outbreak and about the shooting of an unarmed black woman, both in Atlanta—were the work of an organization in Russia called the Internet Research Agency. That organization is just one example of what have come to be known as "troll farms."

Trolling for Clicks

On the internet, a troll is someone who provokes quarrels or upsets people by posting inflammatory messages in a chat room, the comments section of a blog or newspaper, or some other online community. Troll farms, on the other hand, are large, government-run efforts that are intended to create the impression of widespread public support for an issue or political figure. Most closely associated with Russia and the government of President Vladimir Putin, troll farms are powerful tools for spreading fake news on the internet.

Does Fake News Matter?

Fake news can be a prank that someone carries out for his or her own amusement, it can be satire that makes millions of people laugh, or it can be deadly serious. One of the most famous early examples of fake news—that the battleship USS *Maine* had been sunk on purpose rather than by accident—led to war. In 2003, the widespread belief in stories that turned out to be false led to a far more deadly war. In 2016, fake news may even have affected the result of the US presidential election. Clearly, fake news matters. Fighting the spread of fake news is increasingly the job of journalists of all stripes.

In 2002, government officials, particularly in the United States but also in the United Kingdom and Australia, began to warn that the president of Iraq was in the process of developing powerful chemical and nuclear weapons. These were called "weapons of mass destruction," or WMDs for short. The fear that Iraq would soon be able to use those weapons to attack the United State or its allies was the major justification for the US-led invasion of Iraq, which began in March 2003.

The reports about WMDs in Iraq were false. Government officials knew the claims were false, but many journalists were unwilling or unable to challenge the stories. That failure, combined with the use of the internet to amplify the voices of those who advocated for the war against Iraq, led to the most powerful early demonstration of the consequences of fake news in the internet age.

The role of the internet in the way people get their news grew dramatically in the decade after the invasion of Iraq. The amount of intentionally false or misleading

The Economics of Online Journalism

The internet did not cause the decline in print journalism and network newscasts. Those trends were under way before digital technology became widespread. But there is no question that the internet accelerated the shift by fundamentally changing the way news organizations make money.

A crucial element in how newspapers sold advertising was the fact that the paper was something people held in their hands. Subscribers could read the paper from front to back, spending

The internet accelerated the decline in print journalism and network newscasts. That's because the internet fundamentally impacted news organizations' ability to make money, particularly through advertisements.

time on each page, and then share it with others. Few people actually did that—some would read the world news, others the sports section, and others the book reviews—but advertisers relied on that assumption to determine how many people would see their ads. Today, the role of bringing people with varying interests together in one place lies with Google News or the *Huffington Post* or the *Drudge Report*. They give the news away for free. So the economic model has changed on both ends: advertisers are unwilling to pay for the ads, and readers are unwilling to pay for the news.

That does not mean newspapers or newscasts are doomed. It does mean they need to find ways to take advantage of aspects of digital communication that many are just beginning to explore. For example, a key feature of online news sites is that they are inexpensive to create, which means it is a good way to experiment with new features and formats in order to find those that attract the most users. The successful sites will also attract the advertising dollars that no longer flow just to the newspaper publishers. The speed with which reporters and news organizations find and exploit those opportunities will shape the future of online journalism.

WAR SPECIAL

4 STAR **BROOKLYN** FINAL

DAILY ◉ NEWS

50¢   www.nydailynews.com   **NEW YORK'S HOMETOWN NEWSPAPER**   Thursday, March 20, 2003

FIRST STRIKE

GOOD MORNING, BAGHDAD

COVERAGE BEGINS ON PAGES 2-3

The internet amplified support for the war in Iraq, though claims that Iraq had weapons of mass destruction proved false. Both newspapers and websites spread the claims nonetheless.

information that was available grew too. By 2016, not only were most people in the United States getting their news via social media, but purveyors of false stories had become much more sophisticated in exploiting the power and reach of Facebook, Twitter, and other platforms.

Those two trends converged on the 2016 presidential election. There is substantial evidence that the Russian government used official news outlets as well as social media accounts to spread fake news stories that tended to support the candidacy of Donald Trump and oppose that of Hillary Clinton. One detailed analysis by economists at New York University and Stanford found that of 156 fake news stories, 41 favored Clinton and 115 favored Trump, about three times more fake pro-Trump articles than pro-Clinton articles. The pro-Trump articles were shared more often as well: Facebook users shared the pro-Clinton articles 7.6 million times and the pro-Trump articles 30.3 million times.

Those articles represent just a small slice of the vast amount of information and opinion about the election. However, they highlight the problem that journalists now face. Not only do they need to report on events as accurately as possible, they also need to sift through stories that may be newsworthy but also may be malicious. Whether or not the fake news changed the outcome of the election is still unclear. Yet the campaign and the response to it has unquestionably shifted the way journalists do their jobs, and the shift may be profound.

Can We Fight Fake News?

Just after to the 2016 election, President Obama warned Mark Zuckerberg, the founder of Facebook, about the threat of fake news and political disinformation. Zuckerberg reportedly responded that there were few such messages on Facebook, and that there was no easy way to fix the problem. Less than a year later, Zuckerberg said he regretted dismissing the problem.

Facebook began to take steps to screen its content to try to slow the spread of fake news, such as adding new ways to alert people to stories that may be questionable. Google followed suit, assigning more than ten thousand employees to electronically flag articles containing misleading information. But the problem is so big that new technology alone will not be enough to solve it.

The other steps to fighting fake news will take longer but may be more effective. One is for independent journalist to check the accuracy of stories. Organizations already exist that carry out this task, including Snopes.com and Politifact.com. Many newspapers and other media outlets are also devoting more time and resources to fact-checking statements by politicians and other prominent figures as they happen, which can help slow the spread of false or misleading information.

Most important of all, however, will be educating people to be more skeptical about what they find online. That can be difficult, especially because everyone has natural biases. These biases may be political viewpoints or personal tastes, and we want to believe stories that confirm them. Sites like Facebook and Twitter make it easy for people to see only the news they are likely to agree with, regardless of whether it is accurate.

Thinking critically about the news is a vital skill in the effort to reduce the impact of fake news. Digging beneath the top results on a Google search, checking the sources of stories, and refraining from sharing everything we find interesting are steps that can help us navigate the new world of internet journalism.

Chronology

1984 Daily print newspapers reach their peak level of subscribers in the United States.

1991 Tim Berners-Lee creates the first web page.

1993 The first newspaper website launches.

1994 Matthew Drudge starts the *Drudge Report*.

1995 The Oklahoma City bombing results in 168 deaths; coverage of the event is an eary indicator of the strengths and weaknesses of the internet as a platform for reporting on breaking news.

1996 The *New York Times* releases its first electronic edition, on January 22.

1998 Google launches, changing the world (and journalism) forever.

1999 Pyra Labs creates Blogger.

2001 The September 11 terrorist attacks claim nearly three thousand lives; many news websites crash due to increased traffic.

2003 The invasion of Iraq begins; the majority of news publications fail to question the intelligence that led to the invasion.

2005 The *Huffington Post* is launched.

2007 During the Virginia Tech massacre, thirty two students die at the hands of gunman Seung-Hui Cho; blogs help communicate news about the shooting.

2009 Online news surpasses newspapers and radio for the first time.

2010 WikiLeaks releases US diplomatic cables.

2011 Arab Spring demonstrations in Egypt lead to the ouster of President Hosni Mubarak; Western readers can follow the events through real-time updates from protesters on social media.

2012 The *Huffington Post* becomes the first online-only publication to win a Pulitzer Prize.

2014 The *Serial* podcast airs.

2016 Donald Trump tweets about "fake news" for the first time.

Glossary

algorithm A series of steps followed by a computer to complete a task, especially processing data. Facebook and other social media platforms use algorithms to tailor news feeds to an individual's interests and preferences.

America Online (AOL) An online service provider founded in 1989 and one of the early internet pioneers. AOL originally provided a widely used dial-up service, a web portal, email, and instant messaging. In 2000, AOL purchased Time Warner. It was the largest merger in United States history.

ARPANET The Advanced Research Projects Agency Network was the first successful effort to share data and information across widely separated computers. The technologies used to build ARPANET, which launched in 1969, would become the basis for the internet.

blogs A shortened form of the term "weblog," blogs are discussions or informational websites, often run by individuals and focused on specific topics and originally presented as informal, diary-style entries, or "posts." Newer blogs can be more formal and housed on the websites of traditional media companies, newspapers, or academic institutions.

bots Also called web robots or internet bots, bots are software applications that run automated tasks over the internet. Bots can be programmed to gather email addresses and send out unwanted messages, create fake social media accounts, and many other tasks.

browser A web browser is software used to retrieve information on the World Wide Web. Tim Berners-Lee invented the first browser in 1990, but the first to use graphics and thus make the web easy to access was Mosaic, invented by Marc Adreessen in 1993. Today, popular browsers include Safari, Firefox, and Chrome.

bulletin board system (BBS) Before dial-up services like AOL were widely available, and before browsers made using the web simple, many people accessed the internet via a BBS, which provided basic services like email and access to online news to anyone with a telephone line and a modem.

Craigslist A classified advertisements website founded by Craig Newmark in 1995. Most of the ads on Craigslist are free, and the site took much of the classified ad revenue away from traditional newspapers, which hastened their declining profits and circulation in the late 1990s and early 2000s.

dot-com bubble Between 1997 and 2001, millions of people began to use the internet as a source of information and as a place to shop and conduct other business. Many new businesses, known collectively as dot-coms, were founded during this period to take advantage of the rapid growth and the desire of people to invest in internet companies. The boom ended in 2001–2002, as many of the new companies failed.

Huffington Post A news and opinion website founded in 2005 by Arianna Huffington, Andrew Breitbart, Kenneth Lerer, and Jonah Peretti. The site changed its name to *HuffPost* in 2017.

hypertext markup language (HTML) The standard computer language for creating web pages and web applications. HTML is one of the foundations of the World Wide Web.

hypertext transfer protocol (HTTP) The basic instructions for how computers on the internet communicate and respond to various requests. HTTP was invented by Tim Berners-Lee.

leak In journalism, a leak is the unsanctioned release of confidential information to reporters for publication in print, on TV, or online.

PageRank An algorithm Google uses to rank websites in their search results. Named for Larry Page, one of Google's founders, PageRank measures the importance of a web page based on links to that page.

podcast A digital audio file that can be downloaded from the internet. Typically available as a series, subscribers can receive new installments of most podcasts automatically on their computers or mobile devices.

propaganda Presenting information through biased or slanted language in order to influence an audience and further an agenda. Propaganda often presents facts selectively or produces an emotional rather than a rational response to information. It is most commonly associated with material prepared by governments.

tabloid A newspaper whose pages are half the size of those of a standard newspaper, typically dominated by headlines, photographs, and sensational stories.

teletext An early technology for digital news, teletext sends pages of text via broadcast transmission or cables to users' televisions. It was developed in the United Kingdom in the 1970s and remained in wide use until the late 1980s.

troll An internet slang term for a person who posts inflammatory, irrelevant, or false information in online communities such as chat rooms, blogs, or comment sections, with the goal of disrupting normal discussion.

wiki A website that users collaboratively modify directly from their web browser. Wikis run on wiki software, also known as a wiki engine. "Wiki" is a Hawaiian word meaning "quick."

Wikipedia A free online encyclopedia that launched in 2001 that allows anyone to edit articles. Wikipedia is one of the most popular websites on the internet.

Further Information

Books

Hoffman, David. *Citizens Rising: Independent Journalism and the Spread of Democracy*. New York: CUNY Journalism Press, 2013.

King, Elliott. *Free for All: The Internet's Transformation of Journalism*. Evanston, IL: Northwestern University Press, 2010.

Stephens, Mitchell. *Beyond News: The Future of Journalism*. New York: Columbia University Press, 2014.

Websites

Pew Research Center: Journalism & Media
http://www.journalism.org
Explore the latest media news and analysis about the shifting landscape of journalism.

Riptide
https://www.digitalriptide.org

Billed as "an oral history of the epic collision between journalism and digital technology, from 1980 to the present," this website is a project of Harvard's Shorenstein Center on Media, Politics, and Public Policy.

Tutorial: The Transition to Digital Journalism
https://multimedia.journalism.berkeley.edu/tutorials/digital-transform

The UC Berkeley Advanced Media Institute presents an in-depth look at the way the internet has shaped journalism. The site includes graphs, photos, and links and is an incredible resource for research projects.

Videos

"How Is Social Media Changing Journalism?"
https://www.youtube.com/watch?v=-7esKJDZqzQ

The *Atlantic* interviews prominent media figures about the effect social media platforms like Twitter and Facebook have had on reporting.

"The Impact of Twitter on Journalism"
https://www.youtube.com/watch?v=Nl9xl-kAE8A

This video from PBS Digital Studios explains why Twitter has become a valuable tool for journalists.

"The Power of Digital Journalism"
https://www.youtube.com/watch?v=nhrZHRqUaTo

Anita Li, an editor at Mashable, discusses how digital journalism is an important means of making the news more diverse.

Bibliography

Aday, Sean, Henry Farrell, Marc Lynch, John Sides, and Deen Freelon. "Blogs and Bullets II: New Media and Conflict After the Arab Spring." United States Institute of Peace, 2012. https://www.usip.org/sites/default/files/resources/PW80.pdf.

Allan, Stuart. "News on the Web: The Emerging Forms and Practices of Online Journalism." In *Journalism: Critical Issues*, edited by Stuart Allan. New York: Open University Press, 2005.

Allcott, Hunt, and Matthew Gentzkow. "Social Media and Fake News in the 2016 Election." *Journal of Economic Perspectives* 31, 2 (Spring 2017): 211–236. https://web.stanford.edu/~gentzkow/research/fakenews.pdf.

Berners-Lee, Tim. "I Invented the Web. Here Are Three Things We Need to Change to Save It." *Guardian*, March 11, 2017. https://www.theguardian.com/technology/2017/mar/11/tim-berners-lee-web-inventor-save-internet.

Carr, David. "New Orleans Paper Said to Face Deep Cuts and May Cut Back Publication." *New York Times*, May 23, 2012. https://mediadecoder.blogs.nytimes.com/2012/05/23/new-orleans-paper-said-to-face-deep-cuts-and-may-cut-back-on-publication.

Chen, Adrian. "The Agency." *New York Times*, June 2, 2015. https://www.nytimes.com/2015/06/07/magazine/the-agency.html?smid=fb-nytimes&smtyp=cur&_r=0.

———. "The Real Paranoia-Inducing Purpose of Russian Hacks." *New Yorker*, July 27. 2016. https://www.newyorker.com/news/news-desk/the-real-paranoia-inducing-purpose-of-russian-hacks.

Collins, Lauren. "The Oracle: The Many Lives of Arianna Huffington." *New Yorker*, October 13, 2008. https://www.newyorker.com/magazine/2008/10/13/the-oracle-lauren-collins.

Darnton, Robert. "The True History of Fake News." *New York Review of Books*, February 13, 2017. http://www.nybooks.com/daily/2017/02/13/the-true-history-of-fake-news.

Ember, Sydney. "This Is Not Fake News (but Don't Go by the Headline)." *New York Times*, April 3, 2017. https://www.nytimes.com/2017/04/03/education/edlife/fake-news-and-media-literacy.html.

Fallows, James. "How to Save the News." *Atlantic*, June 2010. https://www.theatlantic.com/magazine/archive/2010/06/how-to-save-the-news/308095.

Idle, Nadia, and Alex Nunns. "Tahrir Square Tweet by Tweet." *Guardian*, April 14, 2011. https://www.theguardian.com/world/2011/apr/14/tahrir-square-tweet-egyptian-uprising.

Love, Robert. "Before Jon Stewart." *Columbia Journalism Review*, March/April 2007. http://archives.cjr.org/feature/before_jon_stewart.php.

McClintick, David. "Town Crier for the New Age." *Brill's Content*, November 1998. http://archive.li/Mt4gh.

O'Connell, Pamela Licalzi. "ONLINE DIARY: Taking Refuge on the Internet, a Quilt of Tales and Solace. *New York Times*, September 20, 2001. http://www.nytimes.com/2001/09/20/technology/online-diary-taking-refuge-on-the-internet-a-quilt-of-tales-and-solace.html.

Samuel, Alexandra. "To Fix Fake News, Look to Yellow Journalism." *JSTOR Daily*, November 29, 2016. https://daily.jstor.org/to-fix-fake-news-look-to-yellow-journalism.

Shao, Chengcheng, Giovanni Luca Ciampaglia, Onur Varol, Alessandro Flammini, and Filippo Menczer. "The Spread of Fake News by Social Bots." Indiana University, Bloomington. Retrieved October 1, 2017. https://arxiv.org/pdf/1707.07592.pdf.

Shapiro, Michael. "Six Degrees of Aggregation: How the Huffington Post Ate the Internet." *Columbia Journalism Review*, May/June 2012. http://archives.cjr.org/cover_story/six_degrees_of_aggregation.php.

Soll, Jacob. "The Long and Brutal History of Fake News." *Politico*, December 18, 2016. http://www.politico.

com/magazine/story/2016/12/fake-news-history-long-
violent-214535.

Somaiya, Ravi. "How Facebook Is Changing the Way Its
Users Consume Journalism." *New York Times,* October
26, 2014. https://www.nytimes.com/2014/10/27/
business/media/how-facebook-is-changing-the-way-its-
users-consume-journalism.html?_r=0.

Sutton, Kelsey, and Peter Sterne. "The Fall of Salon.com."
Politico, May 27, 2016. http://www.politico.com/media/
story/2016/05/the-fall-of-saloncom-004551.

Index

About the Author

Jonathan S. Adams has been writing about science, technology, and history for more than twenty-five years. Trained as a journalist, he covered the latest discoveries in medicine and the environment before pursuing a master of science degree. He has written or edited five books on a variety of topics. He lives in the suburbs of Washington, DC.